Paintings by Rolland Golden

KATRINA

DAYS OF TERROR, MONTHS OF ANGUISH

PAINTINGS BY ROLLAND GOLDEN

John R. Kemp

New Orleans Museum of Art

This publication was made possible, in part, through the generosity of Edward and Betty Lou Furash.

2,000 copies of this book were published in conjunction with the exhibition *Katrina—Days of Terror, Months of Anguish: Paintings by Rolland Golden*, organized by the New Orleans Museum of Art and presented November 10, 2007, through February 17, 2008.

Library of Congress Control Number: 2007934328
ISBN 978-0-89494-104-7
Designed by Aisha Champagne, New Orleans Museum of Art
Photography by Judy Cooper, New Orleans, Louisiana
Produced by the Publications Office of the New Orleans Museum of Art, Wanda O'Shello, Coordinator
Printed and bound by MPress, New Orleans, Louisiana

Cover: *Push Came to Shove* (detail, cat. no. 17)
Page 2: *Silent Vigil* (detail, cat. no. 11)
Page 8: *Throw Me a Line, Mister* (detail, cat. no. 3)
Page 15: *Hot Halloween* (detail, cat. no. 21)
Page 18: *Elysian Fields* (detail, cat. no. 7)
Back: *Early Spring Rain Near the Levee* (cat. no. 26)

CONTENTS

PREFACE AND ACKNOWLEDGEMENTS

On August 29, 2005, Hurricane Katrina unleashed its fury on Louisiana and the Mississippi Gulf Coast causing unprecedented destruction. The subsequent flooding of nearly two-thirds of the City of New Orleans multiplied the disaster and forever changed the lives of its citizens. The arts community in New Orleans, strong and vibrant before Katrina, suffered along with the rest of the city. While there was relatively minor damage to arts institutions like the New Orleans Museum of Art, all were closed for months and some were forced to lay off staff. Artists of all types—painters, sculptors, photographers, actors, and musicians who had long found New Orleans a most congenial environment in which to live and work—returned to find their homes, studios, galleries, theaters, and clubs flooded, for many a lifetime's work destroyed.

A number of visual artists immediately began to document and record the destruction of their city. Due to the nature of their media photographers were the first to respond. In addition to the horrific scenes of the storm and its aftermath broadcast around the world by television crews in New Orleans, photographers—both professional and amateur—documented every aspect of the disaster, thereby creating an incredible visual archive for the future. Over six hundred of these compelling images were presented in an exhibition—*Katrina Exposed: A Photographic Reckoning*—at the New Orleans Museum of Art from May 20 to September 17, 2006.

Now just after the second anniversary of the hurricane and flood, NOMA is proud to present this exhibition of the Katrina paintings by Rolland Golden, one of Louisiana's greatest realist painters. As you will learn from reading the artist's moving personal comments about each picture and in John Kemp's insightful essay, Golden began painting the first of these works after returning to the city and touring the most devastated areas. While depressed and pessimistic about the future of the city he loved, Golden was inspired to create this unique body of work as therapy for himself, which now may provide a final catharsis for many New Orleanians who experienced Katrina.

Unlike a photographer who can create images instantaneously, a painter needs time to absorb the vast visual information he has gathered and to filter it through his imagination to create original and unique compositions. Golden recorded scenes from the continuous television coverage of the storm and the rescue efforts, combining these selected news images with photos he later took himself on the deserted streets, together with hundreds of sketches of individuals, destroyed buildings and neighborhoods.

While primarily a landscape painter, in his Katrina pictures Golden has proven himself to be an extraordinary painter of the human figure, capturing the despair and agony of people whose lives were shattered. For me Rolland Golden's Katrina paintings are the most significant body of artwork to result from the storm. They memorialize the valiant struggles of New Orleanians to survive this terrible tragedy, and his paintings give hope for the resurrection and full recovery of one of the most unique cities in our nation.

Of course without the dedicated and tireless effort of Rolland Golden these paintings and this exhibition would not exist. On behalf of the artist, I am happy to acknowledge and thank some of the special individuals who have supported him in his great endeavor. First his wife, Stella, contributed the most in making this exhibition a reality by her tireless efforts and her belief in her husband and his work. Stella, their youngest daughter Lucille, and his brother Donald rode out Katrina with Golden at their home in Folsom, Louisiana, thereby experiencing the full fury of the storm. Lucille, despite losing her New Orleans art gallery after Katrina and dealing with serious health issues, mustered the energy and enthusiasm to help bring this exhibition to fruition. John R. Kemp, distinguish art critic and humanist, who knows Golden's work better than anyone, except for Stella of course, has again written about the artist, combining depth of knowledge, lack of prejudice and great sympathy. Brian Gatewood, who describes himself as a man "from the brambles," is a skilled craftsman who built all of the frames specially designed by the artist for these paintings, with a care and attention to detail that belies his ruggedness. The artist also appreciates the expert efforts of NOMA's staff in the realization of the catalogue and exhibition: Photographer Judy Cooper, Publications Director Wanda O'Shello, Graphic Designer Aisha Champagne, Registrar Paul Tarver, Assistant Registrar Jennifer Ickes, and Preparators Anthony Garma and Tao-nha Hoang—themselves all survivors of Katrina. Finally the artist and the Museum is especially grateful to Edward and Betty Lou Furash of Alexandria, Virginia, longtime friends and supporters of Golden and his work, who generously underwrote the production of this catalogue.

It was only a short time ago in June 2006 when Bill Fagaly, NOMA's former longtime curator of contemporary art, and I visited Rolland and Stella Golden in Folsom to see the first half dozen of his Katrina paintings. Bill and I were bowled over by these compelling compositions and immediately knew that the entire group had to be exhibited at the New Orleans Museum of Art. In the months since, Golden has worked nonstop to complete the twenty-six paintings illustrated in this catalogue. However he tells me that he is not yet finished with this, the most important series of his career and that I should save room in the galleries for a few more paintings that he hopes to complete before the exhibition opens in November. I look forward with tremendous anticipation to the inauguration of an exhibition that I know will be one of the most important that the New Orleans Museum of Art has been privileged to present.

E. John Bullard
The Montine McDaniel Freeman Director
New Orleans Museum of Art

Escape (detail, cat. no. 10)

ROLLAND GOLDEN:
Art in the Ruins

by John R. Kemp

At first glance, *Throw Me a Line, Mister* (cat. no. 3) looks much like a Mardi Gras scene with jubilant carnival revelers standing along a parade route, waiting for approaching floats. Their arms are waving, mouths opened wide, as if shouting pleas to taunting maskers. But look closely. This is not Mardi Gras. It is a human tragedy with desperate people standing on rooftops of destroyed houses surrounded by floodwaters. Their contorted, silhouetted bodies are burned into an intense crimson sunset. Night is fast approaching and the lifeline hanging from the helicopter hovering overhead is their last hope of the day, perhaps the last hope of their lives. *Throw Me a Line, Mister* and the twenty-five or so paintings in this exhibition are filled with Rolland Golden's sorrow for his native city. These apocalyptic images are a nightmare come true.

During the painful days and weeks after Hurricane Katrina slammed southeast Louisiana and the Mississippi Gulf Coast on August 29, 2005, New Orleans drowned as the rest of the world watched in horror the human drama on television. Almost three hundred years of history and a singular culture that Tennessee Williams called "the last frontier of Bohemia" seemed destined to perish under putrid floodwaters. Prophetically, New Orleans had indeed become the city that novelist Walker Percy once described as a "Catholic limbo somewhere between the outer circle of Hell. . . and the inner circle of Purgatory." Life, despair and anguish floated face down in lifeless shadows. Lives were lost; homes and entire neighborhoods were destroyed. Hope seemed to drown that day, too. New Orleanians, trapped by the floodwaters or who had fled to towns and cities all over the nation, wept and wondered if their city would or could survive. Over eighty percent of the city flooded, fifteen hundred people died and, two years later, only half the city's population had returned.

And that did not include the almost total destruction of the nearby Mississippi Gulf Coast.

As politicians and U.S. Army Corps of Engineers officials squabbled over who was at fault for the collapse of the drainage canal floodwalls, a small group of writers such as Douglas Brinkley, Jed Horne, Chris Rose, John Biguenet and Tom Piazza vented their anger and loss in words while a handful of painters worked their way into the ruins to let the destruction and despair speak to their imaginations and art. Painters, sculptors and conceptual artists such as Phil Sandusky, Simon Gunning, Henry Casselli, David Bates, Willie Birch, Ron Bechet, Jacqueline Bishop, Douglas Bourgeois, Jeffery Cook, Dawn Dedeaux, Lin Emery, Mitchell Gaudet, Robert Warrens, Michael Willmon, Rolland Golden and photographers Kathy Anderson, Thomas Dworzak, Debbie Fleming Caffery, David Rae Morris, Tommy Staub and others felt compelled to document the catastrophe as it unfolded or in the weeks following as the true depth of the tragedy became even more evident. Sandusky and a few other painters actually stood among the ruins and painted *en plein air* what they saw and felt. All feared they had lost all they had known. Was the city's singular culture really destroyed? Were the people who created and lived that culture gone forever? Writers and artists needed to express or visualize their fears about the real and mythical. They refused to be paralyzed by uncontrollable events rushing before them. Art became an immediate catharsis almost as vital to the recovery of New Orleans as federal relief aid. Galleries in the city's Art District, French Quarter and along Magazine Street were among the first businesses to reopen and gather their artists who had scattered around the country.

Not all artists, however, had the same inner need to respond immediately to what they saw or experienced. Rolland Golden's came slowly as the images of destruction, despair in people's eyes and anger consumed him. With all of his signature abilities, Golden has created a timeless body of work that will be as much a part of the storm's collective legacy as the gripping television images that angered a nation. Picasso had his *Guernica* in the Spanish Civil War and Golden has his *Katrina* in New Orleans—both unforgiving human tragedies, one manmade and evil, the other natural worsened by folly, both capture human drama and desolation.

To Rolland Harve Golden, born in New Orleans in 1931, Katrina was a desperate and a melancholy homecoming to the city where his career began in the mid-1950s. During his half-century as a professional artist, Golden has painted images of rain-soaked cotton fields and weathered sharecropper shacks in the Mississippi Delta, brilliant New England autumns, hazy Appalachian mountain sunsets, the frenetic streets of New York, twisting blacktop southern roads, languid fields of red poppies in the French countryside and now the despair of Katrina. Through it all, New Orleans has always been the heartbeat of his inspiration. His paintings evoke memories of shared experiences with those who connect to his imagery. The late Louisiana and Mississippi writer Don Lee Keith once described Golden's paintings as an "evasive melody" that touches on the "faintly familiar." Often using Magritte-like surrealism, Golden's images can be tranquil or, as in his Civil War and New Orleans demolition series in the 1970s, sting the imagination. A high point in his career came in 1976, when his work toured the Soviet Union at the invitation of the Institute of Soviet-American Relations in Moscow and the International House in New Orleans. But that is another story.

The Katrina paintings in this exhibition are, in a sense, a requiem for his damaged city. They express his despair for the city's future. They draw you in and demand a personal response. Some, such as *The Other Side of Caution* (cat. no. 5), *Tremé* (cat. no. 4), *Lake Vista Plea* (cat. no. 6), *Desperation* (cat. no. 8), *Elysian Fields—Land of the Gods* (cat. no. 7), *Good Times Past* (cat. no. 14), *Escape from Eden* (cat. no. 12), *Searching for an Up-ramp* (cat. no. 2) and *Heading for the Superdome* (cat. no. 22) are laments to destroyed neighborhoods, panic and hopelessness. Others, including *Hot Halloween* (cat. no. 21), *Home for Thanksgiving* (cat. no. 23), *Christmas Eve* (cat. no. 20) and *July 4th '06* (cat. no. 16), mark the slow, frustrating and painful progress, or lack of progress, in restoring people's homes and lives. "Holidays came and went and everything sat there in ruins," Golden said. "This is the antithesis of joy. It's anything but that." Present everywhere are the dull brownish gray waterlines that cut across houses and buildings and the brownish haze that hung above the city for weeks like a pestilent cloud.

Golden, his wife, Stella, daughter Lucille and his brother Donald rode out the storm in their home near Folsom, in the rural countryside about fifty miles north of New Orleans. "We spent a harrowing night with violent winds and rain; then the tornadoes came and toppled trees like huge toothpicks on our house and cars, completely blocking all roads and literally covering the ground." Since his studio was located on the second floor, he thought over fifty years of work had been destroyed. Not only had the fallen trees not damaged the studio but an unfinished painting of a statue of the Virgin Mary he had once seen in a field in Sunflower County, in the Mississippi Delta, still stood on an easel just as he had left it. They remained in Folsom four days without electricity or outside communications and in the middle of an intense heat wave that followed the storm. After neighbors cut a narrow path through hundreds of downed trees, the Goldens slowly drove away from New Orleans and north to Jackson, Mississippi.

Along the way, Rolland noticed a house facing the road that had been partially crushed by a fallen tree. A man sat silently on what was left of his front porch, watching traffic heading north. An American flag hung limply from the eaves. Three weeks later Golden painted a large watercolor of the scene from memory. "It stuck in my mind. It helped me get through this." After two weeks in Jackson, they drove back to Folsom only to discover entire forests flattened for miles around. Emotionally overwhelmed by the sight, they returned to Jackson the next day. The destruction took its toll. Facing the inevitable, they moved back to Folsom in late October to face whatever was ahead for them. Rolland, now even more despondent and depressed, told his wife he wanted to retire. After three days, he climbed the stairs to clean out his studio. "I saw the Virgin Mary of Sunflower County that I had blocked in on canvas before the storm. As soon as I saw that I said, 'My God, if that's not a Katrina painting.' I just started working and that was the end of my retirement. I got all fired up."

That fire, however, demanded he visit New Orleans and see the devastation first hand. Though the city was still almost totally deserted and uninhabitable, he drove in on September 27, less than a month after the storm, to check his daughter's

Photos taken by Rolland Golden following Hurricane Katrina and used as reference for the painting *Desperation* (cat. no. 8).

art gallery in the French Quarter. He later reflected upon that visit. "The drive was a shock in itself, as the magnitude of the destruction spread out beneath us, as we drove along the elevated expressway within the city." In subsequent trips to the city, he wandered through Faubourg Tremé, Bywater, the French Quarter and Lower 9th Ward, taking photographs and absorbing the real desolation and melancholia, not just what he had seen on the evening news. "I drove alone into some of the areas close to the Quarter," he said one spring afternoon sitting in his studio surrounded by paintings and sketches. "I felt close to Tremé and the area around St. Claude Avenue for I had gone in and out of there for years. I stood on the sidewalk in a neighborhood once teeming with people, activity and sound, greeted by absolute silence. The floodwater was gone, but signs of its effect were everywhere: four to five feet of brown stain covered all that had lain in and beneath it. Levels of water lines clearly revealed its recession; the air itself had a distinct putrid odor; a brown haze hung in the sky like smoke from a distant, burning field."

Eight months after the storm, Golden noted little change. "I have returned several times to New Orleans, much of which still remains devastated. Despite the pitiful condition of numbers of neighborhoods, some people have returned—to live in apparent squalid conditions. The brown has turned a pale tan, the sky once again almost blue, but heat increasing. Except for the foul water, the Lower 9th Ward area remains much as it was the day after the levee broke—houses flattened, rocking chairs or baby carriages stuck high in trees. It's my hope these paintings will help those who see them better understand what occurred and that we continue to suffer, long after Katrina died."

Like bad dreams, these emotionally dark paintings are composites and impressions of actual scenes in the most devastated parts of the city. Because the destruction was so vast, so complete and so profound, these compressed composites were his way to capture the enormity of the devastation in the limited space of a canvas. Essentially, these images reveal not only what he saw but also what he felt. They represent

Graphite sketch by Rolland Golden for the painting *Tremé* (cat no. 4).

Graphite sketch by Rolland Golden for the painting *Clairborne Avenue* (cat no. 1).

everyone lost or living, every destroyed house and neighborhood, every sorrow, every hope. From photographs taken on location, he drew detailed graphite sketches of faces, buildings and scenes that he pieced together into fuller compositions. "Drawings help me position things and get them in their places. They help me get my thoughts together. It goes back to my days with John McCrady." In the mid-1950s, Golden received a classical training in painting from southern regionalist painter and teacher John McCrady, who turned out many other successful artists including Alan Flattmann and Henry Casselli.

In the margins of his composite drawings, Golden often scribbled preliminary titles that reflect first and visceral impressions. In his drawing for the painting *Tremé*, for instance, he noted possible colors he might use in the final painting and the words "Relief on the Way" as a possible title. The relief being the approaching distant rain clouds that might wash away the wreckage and muddy sediment that covered everything. "I did a lot in the Lower 9th Ward because the drama of the imagery was so strong," he said. "But I also wanted to do a landscape about a part of the city I knew so well," he said, as he glanced over to the painting *Tremé*. "Before Katrina, I knew little about the Lower 9th Ward or eastern New Orleans, but I did know Tremé. In the early 1960s, I did a lot of drawings and paintings there, especially when the city was tearing down so much of that old neighborhood to build the so-called cultural center."

In his drawings for the painting *Claiborne Avenue* (cat. no. 1), a flooded view of ravaged homes seen from under the elevated Interstate 10 highway, Golden toyed with titles such as "Forced Out," and "What Man Begins, Nature Completed," or "Fire, rain, flood and stain." Borrowing from the song, "Stormy Monday," he also thought about the next line in the song as a possible title—"Tuesday's Just as Bad." To create the composition, he added an upholstered chair, cushion and traffic light from drawings and photographs taken in other areas. The smoke he had seen earlier on television when a building on the riverfront burned.

Photos taken by Rolland Golden following Hurricane Katrina and used as reference for the paintings *Tremé* and *Claiborne Avenue*.

In *Lessons Lost* (cat. no. 15), perhaps the most intellectually charged painting in the series, Golden symbolizes how the storm and almost citywide flood destroyed the city's educational system. The flooded school bus is obvious, but floating in the water are numbers and letters of the alphabet. Here were the true victims, the children and the uncertain futures they faced in the city. To create this visual message, Golden pieced together images he found throughout the Lower 9th Ward and Faubourg Tremé. The abandoned school bus was in a lot surrounded by storm debris in the Lower 9th and the destroyed houses in Tremé. The upside down street sign, also located in the Lower 9th Ward, reappears in the painting *Christmas Eve* (cat. no. 20).

Christmas Eve was difficult to paint. "It took layer upon layer of color to capture the essence of destruction, neglect and hopelessness I saw in this area of the Lower 9th Ward," Golden said. "I named it *Christmas Eve* because it is the antithesis of Christmas which means hope. I went back there in December 2006 and two-thirds of all the buildings I photographed were gone." *Heading for the Superdome* (cat. no. 22), initially titled "Superdome Bound," is another composite inspired by a woman he saw on television. She was wading through floodwater with a suitcase on her head, wearing what appeared to be a life vest. The water was almost up to her waist. He placed her in a Tremé neighborhood that he had drawn from other photographs and images. He used this same device again in *July 4th '06* (cat. no. 16). During his travels in the Lower 9th Ward, Golden found a small brick church and, in front of the church, a statue of the Madonna and Child, around which someone had draped an American flag. In the painting, he placed that image in front of houses that had totally collapsed. Flowing from the flag's red stripes were streams of blood that swirled in small cyclonic circles like the hurricane that had caused so much pain.

Storm and flood survivors caught by news cameras also influenced *Home for Thanksgiving* (cat. no. 23). Golden saw the two people in the painting in separate news reports. "He was sitting in the Superdome, answering questions and she was in a group of older people at some gathering spot. She had a fascinating face and she was mad. He's had it and you can't blame him." He brought the two together in sketches, added the checkerboard jacket and destroyed houses photographed earlier in the Lower 9th.

Escape (cat. no. 10) is much the same story. In reality, the three women in this painting were not together, but gleaned individually from television. He positioned all three in front of houses he had photographed on Claiborne Avenue. In one woman's arms, he placed a cross because she reminded him of someone he had known years ago in the French Quarter. She promised God that she would carry a cross forever if her son recovered from some dark illness. The son got well and for years

she carried the cross through the Quarter. "I added this figure with the cross because so many people turned to God during Katrina," Golden explained.

Sorrow is evident in every painting. Sometimes it is obvious but in *Arches of Misery* (cat. no. 25), for example, it is implied. Looking out from the arches of the old Circle Grocery on North Claiborne Avenue, one can see a policeman wading through knee-deep brownish floodwater, searching for survivors. Written on the walkway in big, bold, red letters are the words "Please Help." The large shadowy pleading figure on its knees above the arches represents all those who perished and the thousands of pitiful figures who haunted the evening news for weeks. Golden created the painting from photographs taken during a visit to the area. He based the water's depth on the brown watermarks cutting across the arcade wall, and the policeman from a television news report. "I took photographs and added the misery."

Certain paintings represent so many who either drowned in the floodwaters or survived only to find they had lost everything. In *Desperation* (cat. no. 8), an old grief-stricken woman stands, crying as she looks upon her destroyed home. Painted on the flood-ravaged house behind her is the ubiquitous "X" with coded numbers and references to the day rescuers in boats found a drowned body in the ruins. The imagery calls to mind Edvard Munch's iconic painting, *The Scream* (1893), that symbolized the angst of late nineteenth-century Europe. Goldens' scream is New Orleans 2005. In *Hot Halloween* (cat. no. 21), Golden placed a grieving woman before a barricaded background of destroyed houses in the Lower 9th Ward. "This is a refugee coming home for the first time. I put her in the Lower 9th Ward to dramatize what she must have seen or could have seen when she came home. It was certainly a shock when I saw it."

Push Came to Shove (cat. 17) is a composite of images that emphasizes the destruction's enormity. Golden found the car in the Lower 9th Ward with handprints pressed into a mud-covered door panel. In the studio, he intensified the handprints and added impressions of forearms. He also added a tortured

Graphite sketch by Rolland Golden for the painting *The Spirit Returns* (cat no. 18).

face burned into the rusted side mirror. To create the illusion of floodwater sediment and mud, he built up an impasto to create the all too familiar dark muck that covered cars, streets and houses everywhere. The buildings seen through the glassless car door window frame were there and in nearby neighborhoods.

Escape from Eden (cat. no. 12) is no place in particular but symbolic everywhere at the same time. Like Adam and Eve fleeing the Garden of Eden, a man helps a pregnant woman navigate through a narrow flooded path surrounded by absolute destruction. "This was not created from photographs," said Golden, "but from everything I had seen. People thought they were living in paradise before the storm. These two people are facing us as a reminder of how fragile paradise can be."

Like *Escape from Eden, Throw Me a Line, Mister* (cat. no. 3) was pure emotion and a personal response to the terrible human tragedy. "It was a totally created piece," Golden said. "I wanted to capture what I could see, but I also wanted to

capture how I would have felt on a roof all day and all night with water up to the rain gutters, waiting to be rescued. The rescue helicopters stopped at night and I would have had to wait until the next morning. It was hot and children were hungry. The most profound image in my mind was those people on the rooftops holding their hands up to be rescued."

Surrounded by all this misery, Golden at times forces a sense of hope and renewal. *Searching for an Up-ramp* (cat. no. 2) depicts a man and woman arms locked, looking across the floodwaters to an elevated expressway packed with other survivors. To Golden, this represents those moments when desperate people relied upon each other for survival. "People ask me if I will have anything uplifting in the show," he said, as characters in his paintings stacked around his studio stared back at him. "There's not much uplifting in this mess. People suffered. Except for the National Guard and Coast Guard, this storm showed how ill prepared the city, state and federal governments were and how inept everybody seemed to be. People were left to fend for themselves and many had no way to fend."

The painting that most reflects a longed for resurrection is *The Spirit Returns* (cat. no. 18). Here one sees the city's fabled Olympia Brass Band, escorted by jubilant second-liners, marching home joyfully through an abandoned and flooded-out inner city neighborhood. The water is gone but the brownish flood line can be seen half way up the front of the row houses. Windows are broken, doors yawn open and weatherboards hang from rusty nails. Back when the neighborhood was flooded, rescuers in boats painted coded signs on a couple of houses. One read "10/4 Rescued!" and another simply had the infamous "X" with lettering to let other rescue boats know whether or not bodies were found in the house. But on this day, the Olympia Brass Band made its triumphal return to the city with its entourage of black and white followers. Second-liner umbrellas hover about the crowd like bright flowers in a sad and neglected garden. Painted on the umbrellas were little salutations of hope—"We're Back," "New Orleans Will Rise Again" and "Lord, Here We Come!" Even here, images of despair are not far off. A brown mist fills the upper left corner of the canvas. Barely discernable in the haze are the gauzy and ghostly forms of desperate and frantic people on an overpass surrounded by water, waiting and pleading to be rescued.

"I needed to show something that had a breath of life," Golden said, describing how and why he painted *The Spirit Returns*. "But frankly, I don't feel very good about any of this. It was a way of conveying people returning with a lot of spirit and in a typical New Orleans way. They came marching in with a band. In the end, I put in the veil of where they were coming from and where they were. New Orleans is known for its architecture, its food and music, but it's really about people. They make New Orleans what it is. I was trying to concentrate on people."

Like others in the show, *The Spirit Returns* is a composite of sketches made of houses and neighborhoods between St. Claude and Claiborne avenues and Esplanade and the Industrial Canal. "Other parts of the city flooded, too, but I felt more affected by the old houses that were destroyed. I was emotionally attached to them for I lived in old houses like these in the Irish Channel when I was as a child." The overpass scene and rescuers helping the old man he gleaned from endless hours of video taken from the internet. He added the Olympia Brass Band and second-liners from photographs he had taken of a jazz funeral in 1969.

While painting the Katrina series, Golden relived much of the same anger and despair that drove him in the 1970s to paint the destruction of entire city blocks of nineteenth-century buildings in the New Orleans central business district to make way for parking lots and new high rises. "Emotion is easier to capture in difficult times than in good times," he said, his eyes gazing around the studio. "It's like being a masochist and hurting yourself everyday. We express our deepest emotions during times like these. This series was very, very different and more depressing than the Civil War or demolitions series. It was much more personal and I'm in there by myself, living in this depression."

Ironically, the storm and flood reawakened Golden's love for New Orleans. "I was tired of the making-a-living aspect of being an artist," Golden said. "I was ready to retire. It's a constant struggle, but this has inspired me and rekindled my passion for the city. I had lost much of that when I got involved in painting rural scenes, the East Coast and France. What a shame it took such a terrible event to rekindle that passion. It's the crowning work of my career."

The angry faces, loss and resigned despair in Golden's paintings call to mind a scene in James Lee Burke's short story, "Jesus Out to Sea," in a 2006 issue of *Esquire*. As two New Orleans ne'er-do-wells sat on a rooftop, waiting to be rescued from Katrina's floodwaters, they summed up their sorry lives, the music they played, and the musicians they knew. As they talked, a large wood carving with Jesus on the Cross floated by them. One thought to himself: "New Orleans was a poem, man, a song in your heart that never died." To Rolland Golden, the poem lives in his art.

CATALOGUE
OF THE EXHIBITION

The paintings I have produced about Hurricane Katrina is my attempt to express what I experienced, what I saw and what I didn't see, but could mentally visualize.

I was unable to get into New Orleans until September 27, when our daughter Lucille and I drove into the French Quarter to again check on her gallery and apartment. The drive was a shock in itself, as the magnitude of the destruction spread out beneath us, as we drove along the elevated expressway within the city.

The next day, almost exactly one month after Katrina struck, I drove alone into some of the areas close to the Quarter, getting out of the car several times to take photographs as reference for paintings. I stood on the sidewalk in a neighborhood once teeming with people, activity and sound—greeted by absolute silence. The flood water was gone, but signs of its effect were everywhere: four to five feet of brown-stain covered all that had lain in and beneath it. Levels of water lines clearly revealed its recession; the air itself had a distinct putrid odor; a brown haze hung in the sky, like a smoke from a distant, burning field.

Since that day, I have returned several times to New Orleans, much of which still remains devastated, months after the storm. Despite the pitiful condition of numbers of neighborhoods, some people have returned—to live in apparent squalid conditions. The brown has turned a pale tan, the sky once again almost blue, but heat increasing. Except for the foul water, the Lower 9th Ward area remains much as it was the day after the levee broke—houses flattened, rocking chairs or baby carriages stuck high in the trees.

It's my hope these paintings will help those who see them better understand what occurred and that we continue to suffer, long after Katrina died. It will happen again somewhere; let's hope we will be better prepared.

Rolland Golden
May 5, 2006

1
Claiborne Avenue, 2006
Acrylic on canvas
34 x 50 inches
Collection of the Artist

It was a month after the storm before I was able to drive on Claiborne Ave. The depth of the flood water could be seen by the lines it left on the facades of the buildings.

The power and strength of the unscathed elevated expressway super-imposed in front of the damaged buildings emphasizes their fragility. I added the truck, water and chair, as well as the street light with its angle that countered the expressway.

21

8
Desperation, 2006
Acrylic on canvas
36 x 48 inches
Collection of the Artist

My wife, Stella, and daughter Lucille spoke to this lady, videoing the conversation. She lived in the Bywater section and stayed through the storm in her home. I stopped the videotape (several times) to do three quick sketches of her, and then used one of the sketches to place her in front of the destroyed houses.

She becomes a symbol for all the elderly who were trapped during the hurricane. Alone, with nothing but her stained house coat, a handkerchief and her aged body: if she doesn't receive help soon there is only one possibility.

Six Studies for *Desperation*, 2006
Graphite on paper,
10-3/4 x 7-7/8; 9-3/8 x 7-3/4; 10-1/4 x 5-1/4;
9-1/4 x 7-1/4; 7-1/2 x 9-3/4; 10-5/8 x 13-7/8 inches
Collection of the Artist

9
The Morning After the Morning After, 2007
Acrylic on paper
25 x 42 inches
Collection of the Artist

Many people were saved by rescue squads in boats, like the Wild Life and Fisheries man. The two elderly ladies appear to be despondent and reflective, where would their lives go now. Thus, though tired, the man needed to exude strength, vigor and life.

10
Escape, 2006
Acrylic on canvas
40 x 50 inches
Collection of the Artist

The women and child came from three different snippets of television; I put them together walking out of their neighborhood, seeking safety and relief.

The television images, photographs and my knowledge of New Orleans joined to create this vision of people taking their fate into their own hands.

41

11
Silent Vigil, 2006
Acrylic on canvas
40 x 48 inches
Collection of the Artist

This is the painting that started the entire Katrina series. It sat on the easel in my studio until we returned from Jackson, MS, and New York as refugees. It was begun before the storm as a scene of the statue in a cemetery in rural Sunflower County, MS.

I turned it into a New Orleans cemetery, added the water, buildings and mud; it inspired me to keep expressing myself on this tragedy that engulfed us and changed all of our lives.

Color photograph from Sunflower County, Mississippi,
4-15/16 x 6-15/16 inches

Study done before Katrina for *Silent Vigil*, 2005
Acrylic on paper, 7-3/4 x 10-5/8 inches
Collection of the Artist.

initial study for "Silent Vigil"

45

12
Escape from Eden, 2006
Watercolor on paper
30 x 22 inches
Collection of Manuel and Beatrice Zepeda

This painting is entirely a figment of my imagination. I thought not only of
the Lower 9th Ward, but of Slidell and all the Gulf Coast towns crushed by
Katrina. People helping each other during a desperate situation, it is the only good
thing that came from the storm.

13
Helicopter Hands, 2006
Acrylic on canvas
30 x 40 inches
Collection of the Artist

    This painting began with the face of the man, which I saw on television. He then grew into a full figure standing in a flooded doorway. The silhouettes of the arms and hands I had been experimenting with for days; now was the time to use them. I created the window and broken glass in the foreground to heighten the realization of interior damage.

14
Good Times Past, 2006
Watercolor on paper
21 x 29 inches
Collection of Louisiana State University Museum of Art,
Baton Rouge, Louisiana

The old neighborhoods and houses touch me the most in this Katrina malaise of tragedy. It's a personal thing going back to my days as a child and youth in the "Irish Channel," French Quarter and other older parts of the city.

The chairs were on the porch as if in a last conversation, much as my Grandmother often had done. I added the mattress, a ubiquitous object after the storm.

51

15
Lessons Lost, 2006
Acrylic on canvas
40 x 44 inches
Collection of Michael Sartisky, Ph.D.

    Flooding of the school buses was a huge problem for New Orleans; I wanted to find a school bus. During my first trip into the lower 9, I discovered one sitting in an empty lot behind some damaged buildings.

    Its setting wasn't right to convey my thoughts, so I moved it to a street in the Tremé district along with the upside down sign. I flooded the street, added the floating numbers and letters, as well as other things, then I felt it expressed what I wanted.

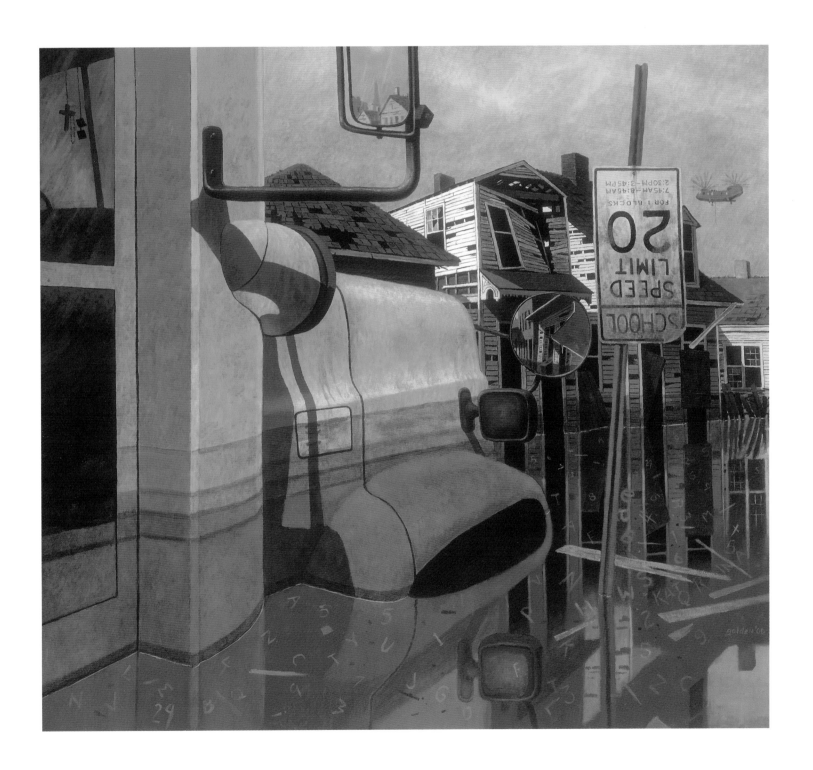

16
July 4th, 2006, 2006
Acrylic on canvas
40 x 50 inches
Collection of Manuel and Beatrice Zepeda

The statue of the Virgin Mary holding Jesus stood in front of a small brick church in the Lower 9th Ward. I decided to superimpose the statue in front of an extremely damaged building, taken from just a few blocks away, to emphasize the irony and hope of this image.

After spreading the red stripes onto the ground to symbolize the bloodshed caused by Katrina, I painted within those stripes swirls emulating a hurricane as seen on radar.

17
Push Came to Shove, 2007
Acrylic on canvas
36 x 44 inches
Collection of the Artist

The car stood abandoned, the door open as you see it. Tumbled buildings stood beyond, smashed by the flood. I rearranged them relatively little. Handprints were on the door, but not as quickly recognizable as in the painting; clearly someone had shoved the door.

I used an acrylic impasto technique to try and capture the muck and mire from which this car had emerged, and hopefully its passengers.

18
The Spirit Returns, 2007
Acrylic on canvas
48 x 60 inches
Collection of the Artist

    After months of venturing into areas of New Orleans ravaged by Katrina, I took heart at the signs of people slowly returning, restoring their homes and lives. To symbolize this life being breathed back into the city, I chose as a subject the traditional New Orleans marching jazz band and the "second line" of people who follow them. Despite the jubilation, strong memories about the suffering wrought by Katrina hover above.

19
St. Tammany Sunset – Post Katrina, 2007
Acrylic on canvas
32 x 41 inches
Collection of the Artist

Of the tremendous devastation in St. Tammany Parish, nature did its best to soften the vision. Sunsets were magnificent, giving the landscape a mysterious appearance; even among the debris of calamity beauty can be found, even if just for a few fleeting moments.

20
Christmas Eve, 2007
Watercolor on paper
42 x 32 inches
Collection of the Artist

I thought this simple house epitomized the sorrowful images that were once the Lower 9th Ward. It was especially poignant during the holiday season, normally a joyous, thankful time. It took several layers of watercolor to reach the degree of muddy filth I sought.

21
Hot Halloween, 2006
Acrylic on canvas
48 x 40 inches
Collection of the Artist

    I tried to imagine the shock the first wave of refugees would have felt upon their return to New Orleans at the sight of devastation before them.

    A brown haze still hung over New Orleans in October; in the most affected areas a strange unpleasant odor joined the haze. I tied Halloween into the painting with the use of black and varying degrees of orange, traditional Halloween colors.

22
Heading for the Superdome, 2007
Acrylic on canvas
44 x 30 inches
Collection of the Artist

A large percentage of people, who stayed in New Orleans for Katrina, did so because they had no choice, no vehicle and no money. This lady has been forced from her home and is trying to reach the refuge "of last resort" as Mayor Nagin called it, the Superdome.

Compositionally, the black suitcase is balanced by the yellow bag; the hanging strap counters the telephone pole, while the outstretched hand breaks this formality and emphasizes her moving forward.

23
Home for Thanksgiving, 2006
Acrylic on canvas
36 x 44 inches
Collection of Renaud and Sonya Rodrigue

These two people came from different television tapes; I stopped the VCR, freezing their faces when I felt they revealed the emotion I was looking for. Returning to one's home to find nothing but rubble is hardly something to be thankful for.

This was one of the more difficult paintings to produce; the last few hours as I refined their expressions were extremely sorrowful.

69

Two Studies for *Home for Thanksgiving,* 2006
Graphite on paper, 9-3/4 x 7-7/8; 10 x 13-7/8 inches
Collection of the Artist

24
Empty Silence, 2006
Acrylic on canvas
40 x 50 inches
Collection of the Artist

    Empty Silence is the second painting produced in this series and is a created scene. Using photographs from different parts of New Orleans, as well as my knowledge of New Orleans architecture, I assembled them together, a typical old New Orleans street.

    The yield sign was taken from an unfinished drawing over thirty years old; it seems appropriately ironic.

25
Arches of Misery, 2007
Acrylic on canvas
32 x 40 inches
Collection of the Artist

I struggled for a title to this piece until I remembered the Arche de Triumphe in Paris; these arches and the situation, to me, expressed the antithesis of triumph. The policeman I sketched from television; the buildings are in the Tremé district near Claiborne Ave.

26
Early Spring Rain Near the Levee, 2007
Watercolor on paper
28 x 42 inches
Collection of the Artist

    I was in the Lower 9th Ward in the first spring after Katrina; it was a dreadful place. The force of the water had shoved houses about like monopoly pieces; some atop roofs or upside down. One house would be shoved into another, merging them like a welder's torch.

    But with the end of winter, as Nature renews itself, hope returns even for those whose lives have been changed forever.

CHRONOLOGY

1931	Born in New Orleans, Louisiana
1934-45	Lived in Granada and Jackson, Mississippi; Montgomery and Birmingham, Alabama
1946	Returned to New Orleans
1950	Graduated from S.J. Peters High, New Orleans, Louisiana
19551-55	Served in the United States Navy aboard four carriers in communications
1955-57	Studied at John McCrady Art School, New Orleans, Louisiana, graduated in June
1957	Began professional art career after graduation; opened Patio Art Studio

Rolland and parents in front of the then Delgado
Museum of Art. New Orleans, Louisiana, 1938.

1957 (continued)

August 31, married Stella Doussan

Exhibitions:
Delgado Museum of Art – Annual exhibition of Art Association of New Orleans, Louisiana
Louisiana State Annual Art Exhibition, Baton Rouge
New Orleans Opera House Association, one-man exhibition, New Orleans, Louisiana

Award:
The Mobile Art Association – "Best in Show," Mobile, Alabama

1958 **Exhibitions:**
Louisiana State Annual Art Exhibition, Baton Rouge
East St. Louis Art Center, one-man exhibition, St. Louis, Illinois
Mobile Art Association, one-man exhibition, Mobile, Alabama

October 2, daughter Carrie Marie is born

1959 **Exhibitions:**
Louisiana State Annual Art Exhibition, Baton Rouge
Downtown Gallery, group exhibition, New Orleans, Louisiana
Gallery Circle Theater, one-man exhibition, New Orleans, Louisiana
Art Association Guild, group exhibition, New Orleans, Louisiana

Commissioned by the Louisiana State Highway Department for fifty paintings of Louisiana scenes

1960 **Exhibition:**
Louisiana State Annual Art Exhibition, Baton Rouge

Rolland with his mother (right) and Aunt
Effie (left) in front of St. Louis Cathedral.
New Orleans, Louisiana, 1938.

Opposite page: Rolland at Jackson Square.
New Orleans, Louisiana, 1938.

79

Rolland in the Cabildo Museum.
New Orleans, Louisiana, 1938.

Rolland, age 8. Irish Channel.
New Orleans, Louisiana, 1939.

1961

Exhibitions:
Louisiana State Annual Art Exhibition, Baton Rouge
Delta Annual Art Exhibition, Arkansas Arts Center, Little Rock
Downtown Gallery, three-man exhibition, New Orleans, Louisiana

May 26, son Mark Damian is born

1961-67

Commissioned by the *Vieux Carré Courier*, New Orleans, Louisiana, to execute sixty-six drawings for the weekly column "Along the Banquette," written by Edith Elliott Long

1962

Exhibitions:
Louisiana State Annual Art Exhibition, Baton Rouge
Art Association Guild, group exhibition, New Orleans, Louisiana
Downtown Gallery, group exhibition, New Orleans, Louisiana

1963

Exhibitions:
Louisiana State Annual Art Exhibition, Baton Rouge
Downtown Gallery, one-man exhibition, New Orleans, Louisiana
Delta Annual Art Exhibition, Arkansas Arts Center, Little Rock

December 11, daughter Lucille Marie is born

1964

Exhibitions:
Louisiana State Annual Art Exhibition, Baton Rouge
The American Watercolor Society, traveling exhibition, New York, New York
Louisiana Art Commission's Regional Exhibition, group exhibition, New Orleans

1964 & 1965

Vincent Price, art connoisseur, purchases sixty works for the Sears Roebuck collection– traveling exhibition

1965

Exhibitions:
Louisiana Art Commission, Old State Capitol, Baton Rouge, one-man, statewide traveling exhibition
California Watercolor Society Annual Exhibition, Los Angeles
Watercolor U.S.A. Society, Springfield Art Museum, Springfield, Missouri
New Orleans Art Association Guild, one-man exhibition, New Orleans, Louisiana
Delta Annual Art Exhibition, Arkansas Arts Center, Little Rock

1965

Awards:
Thomas Hart Benton Award, Watercolor U.S.A. Society
Louisiana State Annual Art Exhibition – Cash Award, Baton Rouge

Elected to Membership in California Watercolor Society

Commission:
Governor John McKeithen, State Office Building, New Orleans, Louisiana

1966   **Exhibitions:**
California Watercolor Society, Los Angeles
U.S.A. Art in the Embassies Program, Washington, D.C.
Watercolor U.S.A. Society, traveling exhibition, Springfield, Missouri
Washington Watercolor Society, Washington, D.C.
National Exhibition of Contemporary Realists Art
Emerson Gallery, one-man exhibition, McLean, Virginia
Bryant Galleries, one-man exhibition, Jackson, Mississippi
Emerson Gallery, one-man exhibition, Washington, D.C.
Americana Galleries, one-man exhibition, Chicago, Illinois

Award:
Grumbacher Purchase Award, California Watercolor Society

1967   **Exhibitions:**
The Butler Institute of American Art, Youngstown, Ohio
American Watercolor Society, traveling exhibition, New York, New York, and,
Springfield Art Museum, Springfield, Missouri
California National Watercolor Society, , Los Angeles
Academic Artists Association Inc, Springfield, Missouri
National Exhibition of Realistic Art, Springfield, Massachusetts
Bryant Galleries, one-man exhibition, Memphis, Tennessee
Life in a Shotgun, one-man exhibition, Bryant Galleries, New Orleans, Louisiana
Down River – Natchez to New Orleans, one-man exhibition, Bryant Galleries, Jackson, Mississippi
Southern Vintage, one-man exhibition, Emerson Gallery, Encino, California

Award:
Horizon City Purchase Award, Gulf States Exhibition, Mobile, Alabama

1968   **Exhibitions:**
La Boetie Gallery, one-man exhibition, New York, New York
Lauren Rogers Museum, one-man show, Laurel, Mississippi
Group Exhibition, Volksfest, Germany
The Butler Institute of American Art, Youngstown, Ohio
Watercolor U.S.A., Springfield, Missouri
California National Watercolor Society, Los Angeles
National Exhibition of Realistic Art, Springfield, Massachusetts
The National Arts Club, New York, New York
Springfield Art Museum, Springfield, Missouri
National Exhibition of Representational Art, Springfield, Massachusetts
Golden Draws Jackson, one-man exhibition, Bryant Galleries, Jackson, Mississippi
Variations on Red, White and Blue, one-man exhibition, Bryant Galleries, New Orleans, Louisiana
Bryant Galleries, one-man exhibition, Memphis, Tennessee

1968   **Award:**
Windsor-Newton Award, California National Watercolor Society

Elected member of Academic Artists Association, Springfield, Massachusetts

Rolland with his aunt Yvonne.
New Orleans, Louisiana.

Rolland with cousin Mavis at Pontchartrain
Beach. New Orleans, Louisiana.

Rolland, age 21. May, 1953.

John McCrady and students at art school.
Rolland is standing behind girl in chair/seated.

1969

Exhibitions:
Watercolor U.S.A., Springfield Museum of Art, Springfield, Missouri
California National Watercolor Society, Los Angeles
The Butler Institute of American Art, Youngstown, Ohio
National Exhibition of Realistic Art, Springfield, Massachusetts
Springfield, Missouri Regional
National Watercolor Competition, Erie, Pennsylvania
Gulf Coast Art Exhibition, Mobile, Alabama
Watercolor U.S.A. Exhibition, Springfield Art Museum, Missouri
Let's Keep Mississippi, one-man exhibition, Bryant Galleries, Jackson, Mississippi

Awards:
Thomas Hart Benton Purchase Award, Watercolor U.S.A.
First National Bank and Sears Roebuck Cash Award, Gulf Coast Art Exhibition

1970

The World of Rolland Golden by Don Lee Keith is published (Royal Publishing Co.)

Exhibitions:
Mainstreams U.S.A., Marietta, Ohio
American Watercolor Society, New York, New York
Watercolor U.S.A., Springfield Art Museum, Missouri
The Butler Institute of American Art, Youngstown, Ohio
California National Watercolor Society Exhibition, Los Angeles
National Academy for California Watercolor
America's Civil War II and II, two one-man exhibitions, Bryant Galleries,
New Orleans, Louisiana
Southern Governor's Conference, one-man exhibition, Biloxi, Mississippi
Mississippi Art Association, *Mississippi Realism* invitational exhibition, Jackson

Awards:
Landmark Purchase Award, Watercolor U.S.A. Society
Cartwheel Cash Award, California National Watercolor Society
Honorary Colonel, Governor's Staff, State of Mississippi

Elected to the following art organizations during this decade: American Watercolor
Society; The National Arts Club; Watercolor U.S.A. Honor Society (past vice-
president); Audubon Artists, Knickerbocker Artists; Allied Artists of America,
Watercolor West; National Society of Painters in Casein and Acrylic

1971

Exhibitions:
Watercolor U.S.A., Springfield Art Museum, Missouri
California National Watercolor Society, Los Angeles and traveling exhibition
American Watercolor Society, New York, New York and traveling exhibition
National Academy for California Watercolor
National Academic Artists Association, Springfield, Massachusetts
National Society of Painters in Casein and Acrylic, New York, New York
Masur Museum of Art, one-man exhibition, Monroe, Louisiana
Louisiana Arts Commission, one-man exhibition, Old State Capitol, Baton Rouge
Delta Variety, one-man exhibition, Bryant Galleries, Jackson, Mississippi

Awards:
Winslow Homer Cash Award, Watercolor U.S.A.
Bruggers Cash Award and Buzza Cordoza Award, California National Watercolor Society

1972   **Exhibitions:**
Watercolor U.S.A., Springfield Art Museum, Missouri
Butler Institute of American Art, Youngstown, Ohio
California National Watercolor Society, Los Angeles and traveling exhibition
The National Arts Club, New York, New York
National Academic Artists Association, Springfield, Massachusetts
National Society of Painters of Casein and Acrylic, New York (January and December.)
Mainstreams, Marietta, Ohio
American Watercolor Society, New York, New York and traveling exhibition
Allied Artists of America, New York, New York
Bryant Galleries, one-man exhibition, New Orleans, Louisiana
Bryant Galleries, one-man exhibition, Houston, Texas

Buzza Cordoza Cash Award, California National Watercolor Society

Rolland and Stella (Doussan) Golden. August 31, 1957.

1973   **Exhibitions:**
Butler Institute of American Art, Youngstown, Ohio
California National Watercolor Society, Los Angeles
Watercolor U.S.A. Society, Springfield Museum of Art, Missouri
The National Arts Club, New York, New York
Watercolor West, California
National Society of Casein and Acrylic, New York, New York
Audubon Artists, New York, New York
Mainstreams U.S.A., Marietta, Ohio

Awards:
Grumbacher Cash Award and Buzza Cordoza Cash Award, California National Watercolor Society
Award of Excellence, Mainstreams U.S.A.

1974   **Exhibitions:**
Butler Institute of American Art, Youngstown, Ohio
Watercolor U.S.A., Springfield Museum of Art, Missouri
The National Arts Club, New York, New York
California National Watercolor Society, Los Angeles
Mainstreams U.S.A., Marietta, Ohio
Audubon Artists, New York, New York
Watercolor West, California, invitational traveling exhibition
Rocky Mountain National Watermedia, Golden, Colorado
Allied Artists of America, New York, New York
National Society of Painters in Acrylic and Casein, New York, New York
Texas Fine Artists Association, Austin, Texas and traveling exhibition
National Academic Artists Association
Watercolor West, Invitational and traveling exhibition
Masur Museum of Art, one-man exhibition, Monroe, Louisiana

Rolland at the Wall of Patio Art Studio. 624 Royal Street. New Orleans, Louisiana, 1964.

Rolland at Vicksburg Battlefield, 1968.

Demolition by Neglect, one-man exhibition, Bryant Galleries, New Orleans, Louisiana
Civil War Drawings, one-man exhibition, Bryant Galleries, New Orleans, Louisiana
Bryant Galleries, one-man exhibition, Jackson, Mississippi
Bryant Galleries, one-man exhibition, Dallas, Texas

Awards:
De Silva Cash Award, California National Watercolor Society
Catok Memorial Award, National Academic Artists Association
Barney Paisner Mem. Award, National Society of Painters in Casein and Acrylic

1975

Exhibitions:
American Watercolor Society, New York, New York and traveling exhibition
National Watercolor Society, Los Angeles, California and traveling exhibition
National Academic Artists Association, Springfield, Massachusetts
Watercolor U.S.A., Springfield Museum of Art, Missouri
National Society of Painters in Casein and Acrylic, New York, New York
American Watercolor Society, New York, New York
Allied Artists of America, New York, New York
Old Bergen Art Guild, traveling exhibition, New Jersey
Heritage and Horizons invitation one-man exhibition, New Orleans, Louisiana
Bryant Galleries, one-man exhibition, New Orleans, Louisiana
Virginia, one-man exhibition, Abbott Galleries, McLean, Virginia

1976

Exhibitions:
U.S.S.R. one-man invitational exhibition, touring Moscow, Leningrad, Kiev and Odessa
The Shack, one-man exhibition, Vincent Mann Gallery, New Orleans, Louisiana
Watercolor U.S.A. Bicentennial Invitational, Springfield Art Museum, Missouri
Mainstreams U.S.A., Marietta, Ohio
National Watercolor Society, Los Angeles, California
Allied Artists of America, New York, New York
National Society of Painters in Casein and Acrylic, New York, New York
Audubon Artists, New York, New York
Portsmouth Community Arts Center, Portsmouth, Virginia
Great Expectations Gallery, one-man exhibition, Memphis, Tennessee
Market Barn Gallery, one-man exhibition, Falmouth, Massachusetts

1976

Listed in Who's Who in American Art

1977

Exhibitions:
The National Arts Club, New York, New York
Butler Institute of American Art, Youngstown, Ohio
Mainstreams U.S.A., Marietta, Ohio
National Academic Artists Association, Springfield, Massachusetts
National Society of Painters in Casein & Acrylic, New York, New York
Civil War Battlefields – Today, one-man exhibition, Masur Museum of Art, Monroe, Louisiana
Civil War Battlefields – Today, one-man exhibition, Crescent Gallery, New Orleans, Louisiana
Natchez Art Association, one-man exhibition, Natchez, Mississippi

Opened Crescent Gallery I, French Quarter

1978   **Exhibitions:**
American Watercolor Society, New York, New York
Butler Institute of American Art, Youngstown, Ohio
Rocky Mountain National Watermedia, Golden, Colorado
Allied Artists of American, New York, New York
The National Arts Club, New York, New York
National Watercolor Society, Los Angeles, California
Salmagundi Club, New York, New York
Civil War Battlefields – Today, one-man exhibition, Old State Capitol,
Jackson, Mississippi
Civil War Battlefields – Today, one-man exhibition, Old State Capitol, Baton
Rouge, Louisiana
Crescent Gallery, one-man exhibition, New Orleans, Louisiana
Market Barn Gallery, one-man exhibition, Falmouth, Massachusetts

Awards:
Paul Remmey Memorial Award, American Watercolor Society
Colorado Watermedia Award, Second Place Award, Rocky Mountain National
Watermedia
Helga Hansen Memorial Award, National Watercolor Society
Second Place Cash Award, The National Arts Club

1979   **Exhibitions:**
Watercolor U.S.A., Springfield Museum of Art, Missouri
National Society of Painters in Casein and Acrylic, New York, New York
Rocky Mountain National Watermedia, Golden, Colorado
National Watercolor Society, Los Angeles, California
Southern Realism, group invitational exhibition, Mississippi Museum of Art, Jackson
Art in Public Places, group exhibition, Louisiana State Arts Council, Old State Capitol,
Baton Rouge, Louisiana
Roads, Streets and Highways, one-man exhibition, Crescent Gallery, New Orleans,
Louisiana

1980   **Exhibitions:**
The National Arts Club, New York, New York
Audubon Artists, New York, New York
Academic Artists Association, Springfield, Massachusetts
National Society of Casein and Acrylic, New York, New York.
Chautauqua Art Association, one-man exhibition, New York
Arts Center of the Ozarks, one-man exhibition, Arkansas
Roads and Highways, one-man exhibition, Crescent Gallery, New Orleans, Louisiana

Awards:
Second Place Award, The National Arts Club
Zinn's, Ltd. Award, Audubon Artists
Graphic Arts of Springfield, Academic Artists Association

1981   **Exhibitions:**
The National Arts Club, New York, New York
National Society of Painters in Casein and Acrylic, New York, New York

Rolland in the studio, on Burgundy Street.
New Orleans, Louisiana. 1970.

Rocky Mountain National Watermedia exhibition, Golden, Colorado
Watercolor West, California
Georgia Watercolor Society, Macon, Georgia
Old State Capitol, group exhibition – John McCrady retrospective and students, Baton Rouge, Louisiana

Awards:
President's Award & honoring with one-man exhibition, The National Arts Club
Art Hardware Award, Rocky Mountain National Watermedia
Grumbacher Silver Medallion and cash Award, Watercolor West
David Soloway Memorial Award, National Society Painters of Casein and Acrylic
Columbus Bank and Trust Award, Georgia Watercolor Society

Closed Crescent Gallery

Rolland at the studio on 1123 Burgundy Street.
New Orleans, Louisiana. September 1971.

1982

Exhibitions:
The National Arts Club, New York, New York
Allied Artists of American, New York, New York
Audubon Artists, New York, New York
Georgia Watercolor Society, Macon, Georgia
Watercolor West, California
The National Arts Club, one-man exhibition given by the President's Award
Creations Gallery, one-man exhibition, New York, New York
Deep South, one-man exhibition, Old Bergen Art Guild, traveling exhibition of fifty U.S. locations through 1987

Awards:
Rebecca Coleman Memorial Award, Georgia Watercolor Society
Honorable Mention, The National Arts Club

1983

Exhibitions:
The National Arts Club, New York, New York
Rocky Mountain National Watermedia, Golden, Colorado
National Society of Painters in Casein and Acrylic, New York, New York
Audubon Artists, New York, New York
Allied Artists of America, New York, New York
Academic Artists Association, Springfield, Massachusetts
San Diego Watercolor Society, California
Southeastern Watercolorists, Deland Museum, Florida
Watercolor West, California
Walker Galleries. one-man exhibition, Jackson, Mississippi
Reinike Gallery, one-man exhibition, New Orleans, Louisiana

Award:
Grumbacher Award, Rocky Mountain National Watermedia

Rolland on Highway 45, between Tupelo
and Columbus, Mississippi. February 1973.

1984

Exhibitions:
The National Arts Club, New York, New York
Rocky Mountain National Watermedia, Golden, Colorado
Allied Artists of America, invitational, New York, New York

Midwest Watercolor Society, Minnesota
Academic Artists Association., Springfield, Massachusetts
Audubon Artists, New York, New York
Watercolor West, California
San Diego Watercolor Society, California
Southeastern Watercolorists, Deland Museum of Art, Florida
Mixed Southern, one-man exhibition, Taylor Clark Galleries, Baton Rouge,
Louisiana

Awards:
First Place Award, The National Arts Club
American Academy of Arts Award, Midwest Watercolor Society
The Art Association Award, Rocky Mountain National Watermedia

1985   **Exhibitions:**
Retrospective exhibition: Eastern Shore Art Center, Fairhope, Alabama;
St. John's Museum of Art, Wilmington, North Carolina; Fayetteville
Museum of Art, North Carolina; Tennessee Valley Art Center, Tuscumbia
Salmagundi Club, New York, New York
The National Arts Club, New York, New York
Watercolor U.S.A., Springfield Art Museum, Missouri
Audubon Artists, New York, New York
Allied Artists of America, New York, New York
National Society of Painters in Casein & Acrylic, New York, New York
Michigan Watercolor Society and traveling exhibition
Watercolor West, California
Mid-West Watercolor Society, Tweed Museum, Duluth, Minnesota
Southeastern Watercolorists, Deland Museum of Art, Florida
Pittsburgh Watercolor Society, Pennsylvania
Combinations, one-man exhibition, Reinike Gallery, New Orleans, Louisiana

Awards:
Michigan Cash Award
Second Place/Skyledge Award, Mid-West Watercolor Society

1986   **Exhibitions:**
The National Arts Club, New York, New York
Salmagundi Club, New York, New York
National Watercolor Society, Los Angeles, California, and traveling exhibition
National Academic Artists, Springfield, Massachusetts
Audubon Artists, New York, New York
National Society of Painters in Casein & Acrylic, New York, New York
Watercolor West, California
Different Worlds, one-man exhibition, The National Arts Club, New York, New York
Capricorn Gallery, one-man exhibition, Natchez, Mississippi

Awards:
Grumbacher Silver Medal and Cash Award, The National Arts Club
Fourth Place Award, The National Arts Club

Rolland with children (left to right) Mark,
Lucille and Carrie. Thanksgiving, 1975.

Rolland in Moscow, 1976.

1987

Exhibitions:
The National Arts Club, New York, New York
The National Arts Club, one-man exhibition, New York, New York.
National Watercolor Society and travel show, Los Angeles, California
Watercolor U.S.A., Springfield Art Museum, Missouri
Rocky Mountain National Watermedia, Golden, Colorado
Audubon Artists, New York, New York
Knickerbocher Artists, New York, New York
Allied Artists of America, New York, New York
Watercolor West, invitational group exhibition, California
National Society of Painters in Casein and Acrylic, New York, New York
Pittsburgh Watercolor Society, Pennsylvania
Uptown Gallery, group exhibition, New York, New York

Awards:
First Place, The National Arts Club
Michael Engel Mem. Award, National Society of Painters in Casein and Acrylic
Pittsburgh Watercolor Society Award, Pittsburgh Watercolor Society

1988

Exhibitions:
The National Arts Club, New York, New York
New England, one-man exhibition, Nahan Galleries, New Orleans, Louisiana
Nahan Galleries, group exhibition, New Orleans, Louisiana
National Society of Painters in Casein and Acrylic, New York, New York
Audubon Artists of America, New York, New York

1989

Exhibitions:
The National Arts Club, New York, New York
Audubon Artists, New York, New York
Watercolor U.S.A., invitational exhibition, Texas
National Watercolor Society, Los Angeles, California
Watercolor West, California
New York, one-man exhibition, Nahan Galleries, New York, New York

Awards:
Second Place Award, Watercolor West
Gloria Benson Stacks Award, Allied Artists of America

1990

Exhibitions:
The National Arts Club, New York, New York
Watercolor U.S. A., Springfield Museum of Art, Missouri
Rocky Mountain National Watermedia, Golden, Colorado
Allied Artists of America, New York, New York
National Watercolor Society, Los Angeles, California
Audubon Artists, New York, New York
Georgia Watercolor Society, Macon Georgia
N.M. Remembers, invitational group exhibition, Downtown Gallery, New Orleans, Louisiana

Awards:
First Prize, The National Arts Club
Springfield Museum of Art Cash Award
Colorado Watermedia Cash Award
Samuel Burton Spence Award, Georgia Watercolor Society

Elected Vice-President of Watercolor U.S.A. Honor Society

1991   **Exhibitions:**
The National Arts Club, one-man exhibition, New York, New York
Watercolor U.S.A. Honor Society, invitational. Springfield, Missouri
The National Arts Club, New York, New York
Audubon Artists, New York, New York
Rocky Mountain National Watermedia, Golden, Colorado
National Watercolor Arizona Artists Alliance, invitational
Allied Artists of America, New York, New York
Georgia Watercolor Society, Macon, Georgia
Bryant Galleries, one-man exhibition, New Orleans, Louisiana
Bryant Galleries, one-man exhibition, Jackson, Mississippi
Downtown Gallery, invitation group exhibition, New Orleans, Louisiana

Award:
Friedlander Memorial Award, Georgia Watercolor Society

1992   **Exhibitions:**
The National Arts Club, New York, New York
Audubon Artists of America, New York, New York
Watercolor U.S.A. Honor Society, Springfield, Missouri
Watercolor West, California
McCrady and Students, group exhibition, Downtown Gallery, New Orleans, Louisiana
Slidell Cultural Center, invitational group exhibition, Slidell, Louisiana
Bryant Gallery, group exhibition, New Orleans, Louisiana

Awards:
First Place, The National Arts Club
Thio and Katherine Hios Award, Audubon Artists of America
Elected Member: American Artists Registry

1993   **Exhibitions:**
The National Arts Club, New York, New York
Watercolor U.S.A. Honor Society, Springfield, Missouri
Audubon Artists, New York, New York
Rocky Mountain National Watermedia, Golden, Colorado
The Arts Club of Washington, one-man exhibition, Washington, D.C.
Bryant Galleries, one-man exhibition, Birmingham, Alabama
Bryant Galleries, one-man exhibition, Atlanta, Georgia
Northshore Realism, group invitation exhibition, St. Tammany Art Association,
Covington, Louisiana
All American, one-man traveling exhibition, Musee Marzelles, Marmande, France;
Galerie Anton, Agen, France

Rolland with children (left to right)
Mark, Lucille and Carrie. May 1989.

Jacques Framonville and Rolland, Grapholith
Atelier, Paris. October 1990.

89

1994   **Exhibitions:**
National Watercolor Society, Los Angeles, California
All American, one-man traveling exhibition, France:
Bon Encontre Cultural Centre; Villeneuve-sur-Lot Cultural Centre; Toulouse Cultural
Centre, Galerie Mediterrannee, Marseille
France, The National Arts Club, one-man exhibition, New York, New York
The St. Tammany Landscape, group invitational exhibition, St. Tammany Art
Association, Covington, Louisiana

Award:
"Strength in Age," Louisiana State University Health Science Center

1995   **Exhibitions:**
State of the Arts 1995, invitational exhibition, Parkland College, Champagne,Illinois
Watercolor U.S.A. Honor Society, Knoxville Museum of Art, Tennessee
Watercolor U.S.A., Springfield Museum of Art, Missouri
National Watercolor Society, Los Angeles, California
St. Tammany Art Association, Louisiana Watercolor Society, group invitational
St. Tammany Museum of Art, one-man exhibition, Covington, Louisiana
Zigler Museum of Art, one-man exhibition, Jennings, Louisiana
France, Encore, The National Arts Club, one-man exhibition, New York, New York.

Award:
Springfield Museum of Art Cash Award, Springfield, Missouri

1996   **Exhibitions:**
Watercolor U.S.A., Springfield Art Museum, Missouri
Georgia Watercolor Society, Macon, Georgia
Meridian Museum of Art, two-person exhibition, Mississippi
Louisiana Artists Working 1930-50's, invitational group exhibition, Downtown Gallery,
New Orleans, Louisiana
Independence Museum, one-man exhibition, Kansas
Coffeyville Center for the Arts, one-man exhibition, Kansas
Hammond Cultural Foundation, invitational group exhibition, Hammond, Louisiana
Louisiana Drawing Exhibition, invitational exhibition, Southeastern Louisiana
University, Hammond, Louisiana
Golden's Folsom studio, one-man exhibition, "Late Afternoon & Evening"

1997   **Exhibitions:**
The National Arts Club, New York, New York
40th Anniversary Exhibition, one-man exhibition, The National Arts Club, New York,
New York
Watercolor U.S.A., Springfield Museum of Art, Missouri
Allied Artists of America, New York, New York
Watercolor '97, invitational exhibition, Hammond Cultural Foundation, Hammond,
Louisiana

Rolland at the National Arts Club studio.
May 1991.

Awards:
Grumbacher Gold Medallion and Cash Award, The National Arts Club
Award of Distinction, "Portrait Inspirations," Rockport Publishing Co.
Award of Distinction: "Creative Inspirations," Rockport Publishing Co.

1998   **Exhibitions:**
The National Arts Club, one-man exhibition, New York, New York
Slidell Cultural Center, one-man exhibition, original lithographs
Boys of the South, group exhibition, Madison Gallery, Madison, Mississippi
Slidell Cultural Center, group exhibition, Louisiana

1999   **Exhibitions:**
Allied Artists of America, New York, New York
Watercolor West, California
FrancoFete '99, two-person traveling exhibition in Louisiana: Louisiana
State University Museum of Art, Baton Rouge, Louisiana; West Baton
Rouge Museum of Art, Port Allen, Louisiana (group show); St. Tammany
Art Association; Taylor Clark Gallery, Baton Rouge, Louisiana; Earthworks, Fine Art
Gallery, Lake Charles, Louisiana
Walton Art Center, one-man exhibition, original lithographs, Arkansas
The 1990's, invitational group exhibition, Meridian Museum of Art, Meridian,
Mississippi
For the 1000th Time, Slidell Cultural Center, group invitation exhibition, Slidell,
Louisiana

            Award:
Ben Rabe Award, "Weird, But Neat," Watercolor West

2000   **Exhibitions:**
Ogden Museum Gallery, exhibition: Michael Brown and Linda Green Collection
Artists of America, group invitational exhibition, Denver, Colorado
The National Arts Club, New York, New York
Watercolor U.S.A. Honor Society, Invitational, Springfield Art Museum, Missouri
Watercolor U.S.A., Springfield Museum of Art, Missouri
The National Arts Club, one-man exhibition, New York, New York
Recent Acquisitions, group exhibition, New Orleans International Airport, Kenner,
Louisiana
Crescent Gallery, one-man exhibition (original lithographs) New Orleans, Louisiana
Crescent Gallery, group exhibition, New Orleans, Louisiana
The McCrady Legacy, group exhibition, St. Tammany Art Association, Covington,
Louisiana

2001   **Exhibitions:**
The National Arts Club, New York, New York
Acquisitions in Prints and Drawings 1996-2000, group exhibition, New Orleans
Museum of Art, New Orleans, Louisiana
Watercolor U.S.A., Springfield Art Museum, Missouri
Butler Institute of American Art, Youngstown, Ohio

National Arts Club. Rolland, E. Raymond Kinetter and
M. Stephen Doherty (editor-in-chief *American Artist*
magazine). August 1992.

Rolland in France. October 1993.

Allied Artists of America, invitational group show, Butler Institute of American Art
Allied Artists of American, New York, New York.
Audubon Artists, New York, New York
Winter Into Spring, one-man exhibition, Crescent Gallery, New Orleans, Louisiana
Crescent Gallery, group exhibition, New Orleans, Louisiana
Reunion, group exhibition, St. Tammany Art Association, Covington, Louisiana

2002   **Exhibitions:**
The National Arts Club, New York, New York
Watercolor U.S.A., Springfield Museum of Art, Missouri
Bradford Britton Museum of Art, invitational exhibition, Big Horn, Wyoming
Shades of Patriotism, group exhibition, Crescent Gallery, New Orleans, Louisiana

Award:
The Salzman Cash Award, The National Arts Club

2003   **Exhibitions:**
Watercolor U.S.A., Springfield Museum of Art, Missouri
Rocky Mountain National Watermedia, Golden, Colorado
National Watercolor Society, Los Angeles, California
The National Arts Club, New York, New York
Allied Artists of America, New York, New York
November in Louisiana and France, one-man exhibition, Crescent Gallery, New Orleans, Louisiana
November in Louisiana and France, one-man exhibition, The National Arts Club, New York, New York
Crescent Gallery, group exhibition, New Orleans, Louisiana

Awards:
The Salzman Award, The National Arts Club

2004   **Exhibitions:**
It's All About the South, one-man exhibition, Crescent Gallery, New Orleans, Louisiana
It's All About the South, one-man exhibition, The National Arts Club, New York, New York

Award:
"Strength in Age," Louisiana State University

2005   **Exhibition:**
The National Arts Club, one-man exhibition, New York, New York

August 29, Hurricane Katrina makes landfall

2006   **Exhibition:**
First Four Katrina Paintings and Related Studies, New Orleans Museum of Art,
New Orleans, Louisiana

Award:
Skyledge Award, Transparent Watercolor Society of America

2007   **Exhibition:**
The Mississippi Story, one-man exhibition, Mississippi Museum of Art, Jackson,
Mississippi
Katrina: Catastrophe and Catharsis, group exhibition, Colorado Springs Fine Arts
Center, Colorado Springs, Colorado
Katrina—Days of Terror, Months of Anguish: Paintings by Rolland Golden,
New Orleans Museum of Art, New Orleans, Louisiana

Listed in Who's Who in America

Rolland in Mississippi. February 2004.

SELECTED PUBLIC COLLECTIONS

Alabama Power Company
Alexandria Museum of Art, Alexandria, Louisiana
Baton Rouge Art Association, Baton Rouge, Louisiana
Bon Encontre Cultural Center, Bon Encontre, France
Chism Bank, Texas
City National Bank of Baton Rouge, Baton Rouge, Louisiana
City of New Orleans, New Orleans, Louisiana
Columbia Pictures, Hollywood, California
Cox Communications, New Orleans,
Deposit Guaranty Bank of Mississippi, Jackson, Mississippi
First National Bank of Commerce, New Orleans, Louisiana
Furash & Co., Washington, D.C.
The Historic New Orleans Collection, New Orleans, Louisiana
Lauren Rogers Museum of Art, Laurel, Mississippi
Louis Armstrong New Orleans International Airport, Kenner, Louisiana
Louisiana's Art in Public Places, Baton Rouge
Louisiana Bank & Trust, Baton Rouge
Louisiana State University Museum of Art, Baton Rouge
Masur Museum of Art, Monroe, Louisiana
Meridian Museum of Art, Meridian, Mississippi
Mississippi Bank, Jackson
Mississippi Museum of Art, Jackson
The National Arts Club, New York, New York
New Orleans Art Association, New Orleans, Louisiana
New Orleans Museum of Art, New Orleans, Louisiana
Ochsner Foundation, Jefferson, Louisiana
Ogden Museum of Southern Art, New Orleans, Louisiana
Pfizer, Inc., New York, New York
Plymouth Savings Bank, Massachusetts
Pushkin Museum, Moscow, Russia
Southeast Louisiana University, Hammond, Louisiana
Springfield Art Museum, Springfield, Missouri
St. John's Museum of Art, Willmington, North Carolina
St. Tammany Justice Center, Covington, Louisiana
Unifirst Bank & Savings, Jackson, Mississippi
University of West Alabama, Livingston, Alabama
Wichita Falls Museum of Art, Wichita Falls, Texas
Zigler Museum of Art, Jennings, Louisiana

SELECTED BIBLIOGRAPHY

BOOKS

Albert, Greg, and Wolfe, Rachel. *Splash-I, America's Best Contemporary Watercolor*. Cincinnati, Ohio: North Light Books, 1991.

Brommer, Gerald. *Transparent Watercolor: Ideas & Techniques*. Worcester, Mass: Davis Publications, Inc., 1973.

Brommer, Gerald. *Understanding Transpaent Watercolor*. Worcester, Mass: Davis Publications, Inc., 1993.

Brommer, Gerald, and Kinne, Nancy. *Exploring Painting*. Worcester, Mass: Davis Publications, Inc.,1988.

Delehanty, Randolph. *Art in the American South: Works from the Roger Ogden Collection*. Baton Rouge, La.: Louisiana State University Press, 1996.

Doherty, M. Stephen. *Developing Ideas in Art Work*. New York, NY: Watson-Guptill, 1998.

Doherty, M. Stephen. *Easy Solutions: Color Mixing*. Gloucester, Mass.: Rockport Publishers, Inc., 1998.

Golden, Rolland. *Rolland Golden: Soviet Touring Exhibit 76/77*. New Orleans, La.: International House/World Trade Center, New Orleans and the Institute of Soviet-American Relations, Moscow, 1977.

Inspirations. Gloucester, Mass.: Rockport Publishers, Inc., 1997.

Kemp, John R. *Rolland Golden: The Journeys of a Southern Artist*. Gretna, La.: Pelican Publishing Company, 2005.

Keith, Don Lee. *The World of Rolland Golden*. New Orleans, La.: Royal Publishing Company, 1970.

Long, Edith Elliott. *Along the Banquette*. New Orleans, La.: Vieux Carré Property Owners, Residents and Associates, Inc., 2004.

Mowbray, Claire. *Exploring Painting*. Worcester, Mass.: Davis Publications, Inc., 1988.

Schlemm, Betty Lou and Hollerbach, Serge. *The Best of Watercolor III*. Gloucester, Mass.: Rockport Publishers, Inc., 1999.

The Best of Acrylic. Rockport, Mass.: Rockport Publishers, Inc., 1996.

The Best of Oil. Rockport, Mass.: Rockport Publishers, Inc., 1996.

Quiller, Stephen, and Whipple, Barbara. *Water Media Processes & Possibilities*. New York, NY: Watson-Guptill, 1986.

"Watercolor and Gouache." *Grumbacher Catalog*. Cranbury, New Jersey: Grumbacher, 1987.

PERIODICALS

Battaglia, Renae. "November in Louisiana and France." *Gulf Coast Arts & Entertainment Review*, March/April, 2003.

Brock, Lynn. "American Through an American's Eyes." *New Orleans Magazine*, June 1977.

Chartier, Peggy. "Rolland Golden – Relationships between Objects and Shapes – Not Always what We Expect." *Inform Art*, Winter 1995

Cover, *Harper's*, July 2007.

Doherty, M. Stephen. "Recent Images, Recent Concerns," *Watercolor*, Fall 1991.

Golden, Rolland. "Watercolor Page." *American Watercolor*, January 1971.

Golden, Rolland. "The Power of Super-Imposition." *Palette Talk*, May/June 1987.

Golden, Rolland. "Creating the Illusion of Depth." *Palette Talk*. September/October 1988.

Gorman, William D. "Rolland Golden's Southland." *Today's Art*, September 1979.

Henriques, Dorothy. "The Golden Touch." *Louisiana Life*, September/October 1982.

Hill, Sarah M. "Road Trips." *Southwest Art*, May 2002.

Keith, Don Lee. "The Golden Boy of Watercolor." *Delta Review*, November 1969.

Kemp, John R. "The Golden Touch." *New Orleans Magazine*, November 1985.

Kemp, John R. "Superimposing the South." *Mississippi Magazine*, July/August 1986.

Kemp, John R. "Collectibles: Fifteen Louisiana Artists." *Louisiana Life*, Spring 1996.

Kemp, John R. "The Golden Touch." *Watercolor*, Spring 2000.

Kemp, John R. "A Feeling of Space." *Louisiana Life*, Summer 2003.

Kemp, John R. "Rolland Golden: The Journeys of a Southern Artist." *Louisiana Cultural Vistas*, Fall 2006.

Kinstler, Peggy. "Imagination. . . Where It Can Lead." *Inform Art*, Winter 2000.

Landry, Jamey. "Rolland on the Villa." *Inside Northshore*, June/July 2003.

MacCormack, Ed. "Story, Space and Structure in the Art of Rolland Golden." *Artspeak*, March 1989.

Marcus, Stanley. "The Artist Engage." *American Artist*, June 1985.

Menan, Chandra. "Winter into Spring." *Gulf Coast Arts and Entertainment Review*, November/December 2001.

Michaels, Dorothy. "From a Distant Shore." *Watercolor*, Fall 1995.

Rase, Stacey. "Art Abounding." *Inside Northshore*, September 2005.

Reed, Harry. "The Results of Deliberate, Intellectual Thoughts." *Southwest Art*, May 1978.

Reed, Harry. "Rolland Golden – New Orleans, Louisiana." *Art Voices South*, March/April 1979.

Simon, Sean. "Golden Returns with Metaphysics of Everyday." *Artspeak*, November 1997.

Sinclair, Joseph David. "Rolland Golden – Questions with Indescribable Answers." *International Fine Art Collector*, September 1991.

TELEVISION DOCUMENTARIES

WWL (New Orleans), Profile, 1967, Bill Elder, narrator.
WWL (New Orleans), Profile, 1969, Bill Elder, narrator.
WDSU (New Orleans), "Rolland Golden's Southland," 1973, Jim Keyser, narrator.
WGNO (New Orleans), "First Person," 1986, Mel Leavitt, narrator.
WYES 1987 (New Orleans public television) feature.
ETV (Mississippi), Profile, 1991.
Louisiana Public Broadcasting (Baton Rouge), Interview, 2006.